Sewing Skills

for boys and girls

Alison McNicol

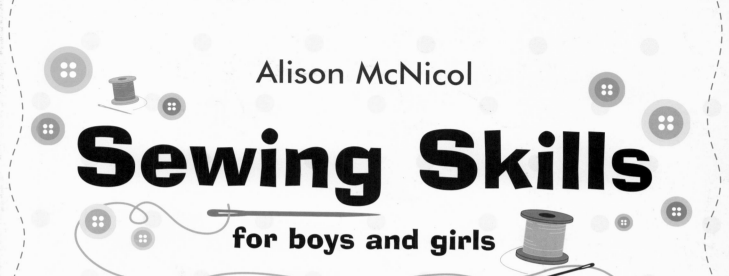

Sewing Skills

for boys and girls

Learn to sew and make 20 fun projects!

COATS

Coats
Crafts UK
Where ideas live

A Coats publication

First published in 2009 by Coats Crafts UK
Lingfield Point
McMullen Road
Darlington
DL1 1YJ

Copyright © 2009 Coats Crafts UK
Text and illustration copyright © 2009 Alison McNicol

Designer Julie Anson
Editor Susan Berry
Photography John Heseltine
Styling Susan Berry
Artworks/illustrations Julie Anson

British Library Cataloguing in Publication Data
A catalogue of this book is available from the British Library.
ISBN 978-1-906007-67-6

Reproduced and printed in China

Contents

Introduction 7

Your sewing kit 8

Skills 10

Stitches 18

Things to make 26
Draughty Dog 28
Crazy Creatures 30
Flower Brooch 32
Bear Blanket 34
Bear Hot-water Bottle Cover 36
Yummy Cushions 38
Hanging Hearts 40
Cool Zip Cases 42
Denim Bag 44
Tissue Monsters 46
House Needlecase 48
Birdy Garland 50
Snuggly Slippers 52
Book Cover 54
Bags of Fun 56
Titchy Teddy Bear 58
Titchy Teddy Clothes 60
Cupcake Pincushion 62
Gingerbread Men 64
Egg Cosies 66

Patterns 68
Suppliers & products 78
Index 79
Acknowledgments 80

Alison and members of Stitchclub

Sewing Skills for boys and girls

Hi there!

When I was a little girl I loved to make things and couldn't wait for my gran to teach me to sew. I would spend hours in my bedroom designing outfits for my teddy bears from scraps of fabric, sewing presents for my friends and family and cool things for my room.

Even though I'm now a "grown up", not much has changed. I still love to sew cool stuff, and when I realised that not many children are taught sewing in school any more, and may not have a grandma nearby to teach them, I decided to try to show as many boys and girls as possible how cool and easy sewing can be — it's not just for old ladies y'know!

I started my first Stitchclub sewing club weeks later, and I knew I was doing the right thing when one of my pupils said "Stitchclub is my favourite club EVER, I love sewing"! There are now lots of Stitchclubs all over the world, and we've taught thousands of children how to sew with our easy illustrations and instructions and super cool sewing projects.

I'm so excited to share my first book with you. My friends Daisy Doublestitch and Billy Bobbin will help you get started and show you just how easy it is to learn to sew… I know you're going to have SEW much fun!

Alison McNicol

Your sewing kit

Before you can start sewing, there are a few things you'll need, and it's a good idea to have a sewing box to keep all these bits and bobs in — that way you'll know where to find everything when you start a new project. There are lots of lovely sewing boxes out there, but even an old biscuit tin or ice cream tub will do.

I also like to keep a separate box or bag for all my bits of fabric and ribbons so they won't get tangled up with pins and threads.

Be very careful with sharp scissors, and always keep pins and needles in a pincushion or a scrap piece of felt when you're not using them, and if there are younger children around, be sure to keep these sharp items well out of reach.

Tape measure
Keep one handy for taking measurements.

Coats sewing thread
Use this thread for sewing things up or sewing on buttons and beads.

Scissors
Have one pair for cutting paper patterns, and another sharp pair for cutting thread and fabric.

Anchor embroidery thread
This thicker thread is great for decorative stitches and blanket stitch. Use a needle with a larger eye.

Ribbons and trims
You can never have too many ribbons and trims in your sewing box!

Buttons and beads
Start collecting these to use in lots of projects.

Needles and pins
Keep these safely in a pincushion when not in use. You will need different sizes of needles for different types of thread.

Fabrics and felt
We use felt in a lot of projects in this book, plus some cotton fabrics for appliqué.

Skills

There are quite a few different sewing skills to learn to help get you started. The more you practise these — like threading your needle — the easier they will become! You can use skills like appliqué and sewing on a button for LOADS of different projects...are you ready to get started?

How to...
Thread your needle

How to choose thread and how to thread a needle are the very first things you must learn when sewing! Threads come in all colours and thicknesses, and needles come in all different sizes for different jobs.

STEP 1

Choose a needle that's right for the thread and fabric you're using. The hole for the thread is called the **eye**. Is it big enough for your thread? Is the needle sharp enough to pass through your fabric easily?

STEP 2

"How much thread should I use?" With the bobbin in one hand and the end in the other, unwind until your arms are outstretched, then *cut*. Always use this amount, even for a small job, as you don't want to run out too soon!

STEP 3

Hold your needle just below the **eye**. Rest your wrist on the edge of the table to help keep your hand steady. In the other hand, hold your thread, close to the end. If it's a bit fluffy, snip the end to blunt it, and wet it. Pass the thread carefully through the eye.

STEP 4

Pull one end of the thread through the needle until the thread is the same length on both sides (unless you're using fat embroidery thread). Tie a knot at the very end and smooth both strands of thread together.

How to...
Sew on a button

Sewing on buttons is easy when you know how!
You can use buttons on your clothes, or even to decorate things!

STEP 1
Decide where you want your button to be and bring your needle up through the middle of that area from the back of the fabric, so that your knot is hidden at the back.

STEP 2
Now make a double backstitch to secure your thread on the fabric **before** you add the button.

You use a double backstitch for LOTS of different things!

Make sure your needle does the in and the out move in one go.

STEP 3
Now bring your needle and all the thread **up** through one hole of the button. Next go **down** through the other hole, again pulling thread all the way. Do this at least 4 times or until the button no longer feels wobbly when you tug it.

STEP 4
On the underside of the fabric, underneath the button, do another tiny double backstitch and you are finished!

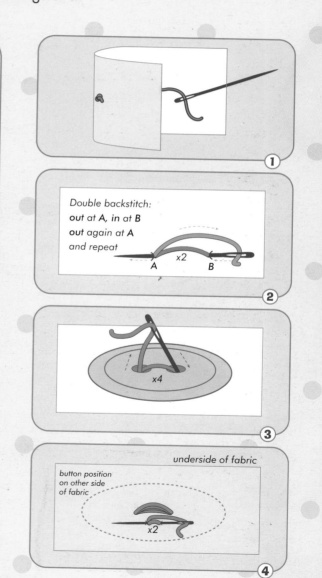

①

Double backstitch:
out at A, **in** at B
out again at A
and repeat

A x2 B

②

x4

③

underside of fabric

button position
on other side
of fabric

x2

④

How to...
Use pins

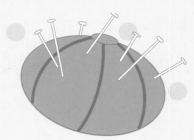

You use pins to attach patterns to your fabric before you cut it, or to hold your fabrics in place as you sew.

STEP 1
When pinning a pattern to your fabric, you must use lots of pins all around the outside of the pattern to hold the paper shape to the fabric.

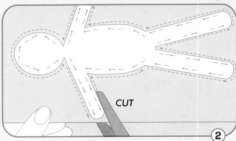

STEP 2
Now the pattern is secure enough for you to cut out a neat shape.

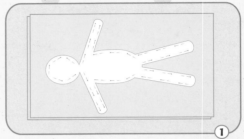

CUT

Tip!

Make sure your fabrics stay flat when you pin them. Check they're not bumpy before you cut!

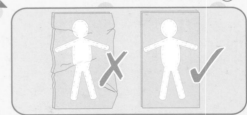

STEP 3
Once you have cut out your shape, you need to remove the pins and paper, and then pin your fabrics back together. This holds it in position while you sew. Now you can sew it together!

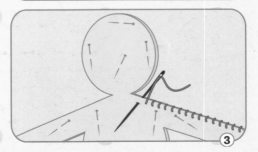

How to...
Use a pattern

You use paper patterns or templates to help cut the correct shapes or pieces for the project you are making.

STEP 1
The paper pattern has a solid line to show you where to cut around the paper pattern, and the number will tell you how many of this shape to cut. First cut out the paper shape carefully. Be careful not to cut inside any lines.

STEP 2
You must then pin the shape carefully to your fabric. Be sure not to waste fabric so think about how you position each shape.

STEP 3
Cut out your fabric shapes, remove the paper, and pin them back together ready for sewing.

STEP 4
On some patterns the *dotted lines* show you where to sew and the Daisy heads show you where to *begin* and *end*. You can use a pencil to mark these on your fabric.

When you see me, don't forget to always begin and end with a double stitch!

How to...
Appliqué

Appliqué (pronounced ah–plee–kay) is a **design** or a **picture** made out of smaller pieces of fabric sewn onto a bigger one — like on a bag or a t-shirt. You can sew **appliqué** either by hand or on a sewing machine. You can also use different stitches, buttons and beads on your "picture"!

STEP 1
Decide what picture or shape you want to use and draw it onto tracing paper. Start off with a simple design until you get the hang of it! You can make it in sections, too.

STEP 2
Cut out each section of the paper shape and pin it to the fabric you've chosen.

Ask an adult to iron your fabric first if it's wrinkled!

STEP 3
Carefully cut out each piece of fabric then remove your paper templates.

STEP 4
Position it on the base fabric and pin in place. Now sew each piece into place with Straight Stitch or Blanket Stitch (see pages 20–21). You can even use different stitches for each section!

How to...
Sew on beads

You can use beautiful beads to decorate things you make, or even jazz up your existing clothes! You must sew them on carefully so they won't fall off when you wear or wash something!

Tip! Check your needle fits through your beads first!

STEP 1

It may help to draw your design first. Bring your needle up from the back of the fabric where you want to start, so that your knot is hidden. Secure your thread with a tiny double stitch which your first bead will hide.

STEP 2 (the right way!)

Thread your needle through the first bead and pull the bead all the way down to the fabric. Now put your needle back into the fabric, just underneath the bead. When you pull the thread through, it will disappear under the bead!

STEP 3 (the wrong way!)

But...if you put your needle back in too far away from your bead, you will see the thread, which will look messy!

STEP 4

Bring the needle up right beside the first bead, thread your second bead and go take the needle back down just underneath it again. Keep going, following your design.

To finish, do a tiny double stitch on the back of the fabric, HIDDEN under the last bead

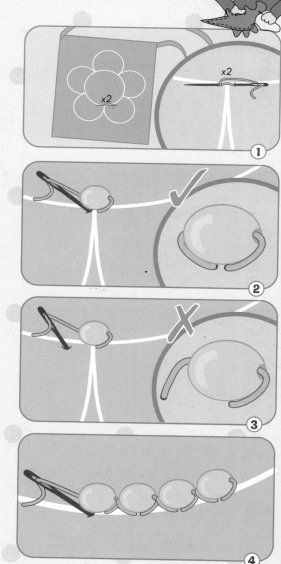

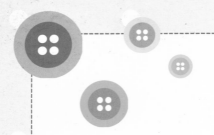

Stitches

There are lots of different sewing stitches to learn, and you will need to use different kinds for each project.

Some of the stitches may seem a little bit tricky at first, so it's a good idea to practise them on some scrap felt before you begin your project. Look out for Billy or Daisy giving you handy tips along the way! Ready?

Let's sew!

How to sew...
Straight Stitch

Straight Stitch (sometimes called Running Stitch) looks a dotted line. It is the easiest of all the stitches and can be used to join 2 pieces of fabric together, or even to "draw" shapes for decoration.

STEP 1

To start, bring your needle up from the underside of the fabric, then pull it all the way until you feel the knot tug. Then, a little way along, push the needle **down** through the fabric and pull all the way. Now you've made your first stitch! To secure your stitching, you always *begin* and *end* with a *double stitch* where you do 2 stitches on top of each other.

STEP 2

Now you can keep sewing — *up*, *down*, *up*, *down, and so on.* Make sure all your stitches are the same size and the same distance apart!

STEP 3

When you are ready to finish sewing, remember to do a *double stitch* at the end.

Tip!

For a quicker way of sewing Straight Stitch you can "weave" your needle in and out to do a couple of stitches at a time!

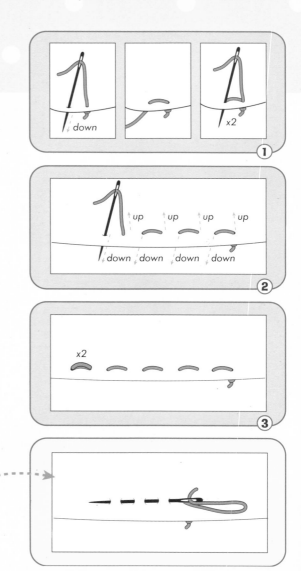

How to sew...
Blanket Stitch

Blanket Stitch is a traditional embroidery stitch used to decorate fabric edges. It works particularly well with felt or fleece, and looks great on cushions, scarves and lots more!

STEP 1

Thread a length of thick cotton or embroidery thread through a large-eyed or yarn needle. Secure the thread with a knot on the back of the fabric very near the edge and make a tiny stitch.

Don't forget to tie a knot!

STEP 2

With the front of the fabric facing you, insert the needle downwards through the fabric along an imaginary line running parallel to the edge.

STEP 3

Loop the thread under the needle point, then pull the needle through the fabric completely. Pull the thread to make a snug stitch along the edge of the fabric.

STEP 4

Repeat this process along the edge of the fabric and secure with a knot at the end.

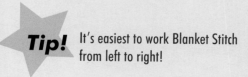

Tip! It's easiest to work Blanket Stitch from left to right!

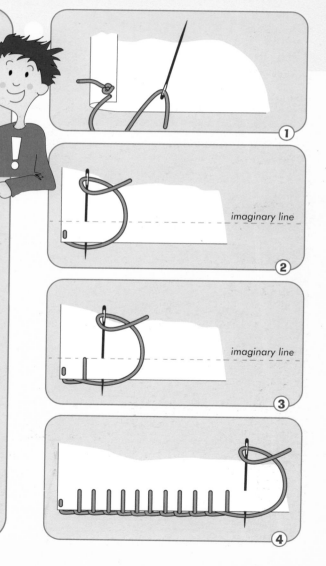

How to sew...
Backstitch

Backstitch is the strongest hand stitch. It can be used to sew pieces of fabric together securely. Backstitch is like a dance — one step **back,** then two steps **forward**. Are you ready to dance?

STEP 1

Tie a knot in the end of your thread, then insert your needle up from the back of your fabric at *A*. Move your needle **back** to *B* and insert it. Bring it forward underneath the fabric and out the front at *C*, in one smooth scoop.

STEP 2

Pull the thread through then go **back** and insert needle again at *A*.

One step back, two steps forward!

STEP 3

Bring the needle forward and out at *D*. So, you go **back** for one stitch to fill in the gap. Then bring it out one stitch **forward** to make a new gap. Continue backstitching by repeating Steps 1 and 2.

STEP 4

For your last stitch, go back to fill in the gap from *G* to *F*, but then only go one step **forward** to come back out again at *G*. Go back in again at *F* and out again at *G* to make a **double stitch** to secure the end.

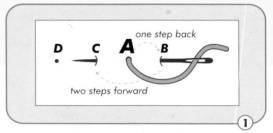

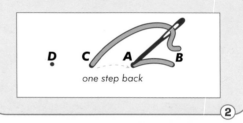

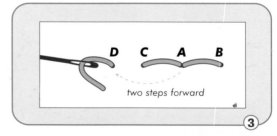

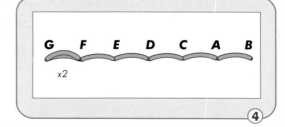

How to sew...
Overstitch & Slipstitch

Overstitch is a very easy stitch and can be used instead of Straight or Blanket Stitch to sew 2 layers together, or to close up gaps in a stuffed toy or pillow.

STEP 1
First, hide your knot by putting your needle in *between* the 2 layers of fabric and bringing it out where your first stitch will start.

STEP 2
Now loop around and bring your needle through the 2 layers and back out through the same spot. Do this twice to start, then move your needle up a bit each time to make a new stitch. Finish with a double stitch.

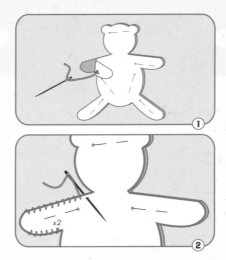

Slipstitch — For stuffed toys or pillows sewn on a machine or in backstitch, then turned inside out and stuffed, you can use tiny slipstitches to close up the gap very neatly.

STEP 1
First start at one end of the gap and bring your needle from the *inside* of the gap and pull it all the way to the *outside*. This will hide your knot!

STEP 2
Now bring your needle from the *inside* of the piece of fabric, *side 2*, and pull through to the *outside* like a zigzag! Continue with tiny slip stitches — inside to out, *side 1*, inside to out, *side 2* and so on, all along the gap.

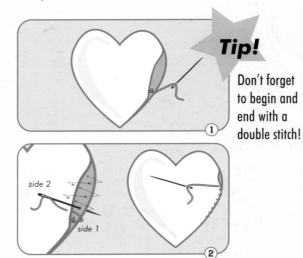

Tip!

Don't forget to begin and end with a double stitch!

How to sew...
Cross Stitch

A Cross Stitch is **2** diagonal stitches that make an X inside a square and can be used to make letters and patterns on fabric! It helps to use checked gingham fabric to help you learn Cross Stitch.

STEP 1
In pencil, mark on the squares of your fabric the pattern you would like to stitch. (To stitch letters, you will need a graph paper chart).

Tip! Remember to tie a knot in your thread to start!

STEP 2
Bring your needle up in one corner of the first square of the pattern. First make **1** diagonal stitch in each of the squares of the first row. Then complete the remaining rows.

STEP 3
When all of the *first* diagonal stitches of the pattern are done, you can sew your *second* diagonal stitches to make an *X*, row by row, over the first diagonal stitches of the pattern.

STEP 4
After your last stitch, bring your needle to the back of the fabric and weave your needle through the threads of the last few stitches before cutting.

Do you have enough thread for the next letter?

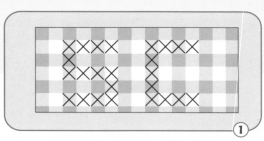
②

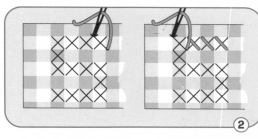
③

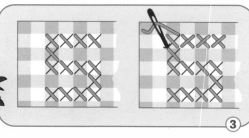
back of fabric
④

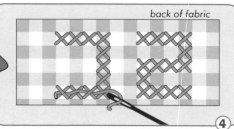
①

How to sew...
Chain Stitch

Chain Stitch is a fun stitch to sew! It is great for making shapes and designs and looks very pretty! You will need to use an embroidery or wool thread.

STEP 1
Start by pulling your needle through the fabric. from the back. With your thumb, hold the thread against the fabric below where the needle first came out. Loop your needle and thread around to the *right*.

STEP 2
Insert the needle where it first came out, and bring it back out a short distance away. Pull the thread through, making sure the thread loop stays tucked under your needle. Pull your thread all the way to make the first link in your chain!

STEP 3
For the next link, make another loop like you did in Step 1. Then insert your needle inside the last link, next to where the thread came out, and bring it back out a little further along, again making sure the thread loop stays tucked under the needle. Pull.

STEP 4
Keep stitching until you have all the chain links you want. To finish, on the back of the fabric, weave your needle and thread through the back of the last few stitches to secure it before cutting.

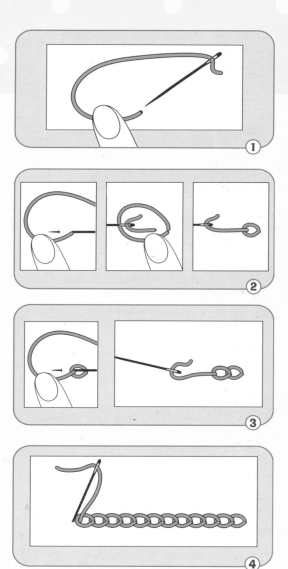

Things to make

Now that you've mastered your Skills and Stitches you can make just about anything! Here are 20 fun projects to get you started — some for you and some for your room — from little teddies to cosy slippers. Before you start, remember to put all the things you will need into a little bag or work box. Many of the projects use patterns. These are shown on pp 68–77. You can enlarge them on a photocopier to the size you want.

Which project will you make first?

Draughty Dog

Stitches: Backstitch, Overstitch
Skills: Using a pattern, using pins
Materials: Fabric for dog, ears and tail, buttons or googly eyes, stuffing

STEP 1

Cut a strip of fabric 25cm/10in wide, and as long as you want your dog to be. Fold your fabric strip so that the *right side* is on the inside and the two long sides are touching. Use the dog's head pattern (p.75) at one end of your strip to cut the curved end for his head!

STEP 2

Using Backstitch, sew about 1cm/½in in from the edge from the tail to the end of the nose. Remember to begin and end with a double stitch. Leave the tail end open so that you can turn it right side out and stuff it.

STEP 3

Now turn your dog tube right side out. Poke a pencil into it from the inside so that the nose part is nice and pointy! Stuff your dog with used paper or even cut up carrier bags. Once he is stuffed full, sew up the end with small Overstitches.

STEP 4

Now cut the eyes, nose, ears and tail from the felt using the patterns provided. Sew these on to give your dog his personality. Now he's ready to be your new pet. What will you call him?

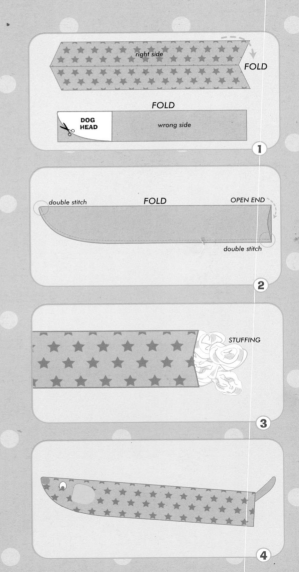

Crazy Creatures

Stitches: Straight Stitch, Cross Stitch
Skills: Using a pattern, using pins, appliqué
Materials: Felt, scraps of fabric, buttons and stuffing

STEP 1

Draw your very own crazy creature on a piece of paper to make a pattern, pin the pattern to 2 layers of felt and cut out.

STEP 2

Now cut out fabric for his eyes, mouth and teeth and sew onto 1 of the pieces of his body. You can use all sorts of stitches to make scars or tummy buttons, or to decorate their eyes and mouths!

STEP 3

Pin and sew the 2 body parts together, but remember to leave a small gap for you to stuff your creature. Once stuffed, finish sewing up.

STEP 4

You can also make small aliens and creatures to use as bag charms and keychains — just sew on some ribbon or a keychain to the back of his head. How many different crazy creatures can you create?

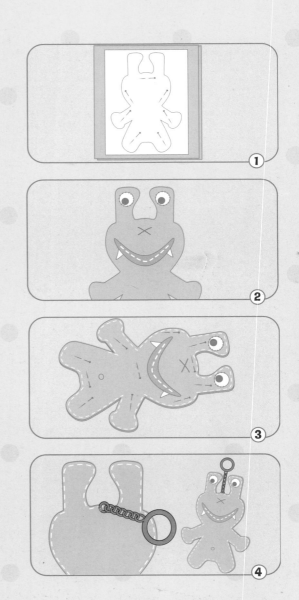

Flower Brooch

Stitches: Straight Stitch, Overstitch
Skills: Using a pattern, using pins, sewing on a button
Materials: Various felts, fabrics, ribbons and buttons, safety or brooch pin

STEP 1

Cut out your flower shape (p.72) from a piece of felt. This will form the back of your brooch. Now cut out lots of leaf shapes from different coloured or patterned fabrics.

STEP 2

Start sewing the leaf shapes onto the felt backing, with your stitches all being hidden in the middle of the flower. Add as many leaves as you like until you have made a pretty flower.

STEP 3

Then sew a button onto the middle of the brooch to hide all the stitches. You can also add beads or stitches to some of the leaves to make them pretty.

These brooches make a great birthday present for a friend

STEP 4

Now Overstitch a brooch pin or safety pin to the back of the brooch felt. Your brooch is now ready to wear! Why not make one for every outfit?

Bear Blanket

Stitches: Blanket Stitch, Straight Stitch
Skills: Using a pattern, using pins, sewing on a button, appliqué
Materials: Furry or fleece fabric for blanket, fabric for bear face and paws, thick embroidery thread

STEP 1

Take a large, plain blanket, or cut a large piece of fleece or furry fabric. Using thick thread, sew all around the edges with Blanket Stitch.

Now I know why they call it Blanket Stitch!

STEP 2

Use the patterns (p.77) to cut out the bear head and paws from the other piece of fabric.

STEP 3

Sew your bear ears to your bear face with Straight Stitch, add buttons or felt for his eyes, and stitch his muzzle in Straight Stitch.

STEP 4

Now sew your bear and his paws onto one corner of the blanket! Are you ready to make the matching hot-water bottle cover on the next page?

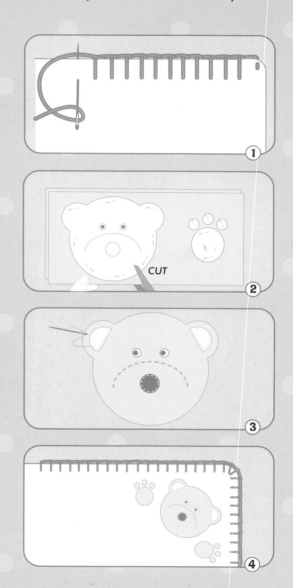

Bear Hot-water Bottle Cover

Stitches: Blanket Stitch, Straight Stitch
Skills: Using a pattern, using pins, sewing on a button, appliqué
Materials: Furry or fleece fabric for bottle cover, fabric for bear face and paws, embroidery thread

STEP 1

Draw around your hot-water bottle to make a paper template, adding a 2cm/³⁄₄in border all the way around to allow enough fabric for sewing.

STEP 2

Use this template to cut out 1 panel for the front of your cover and 2 back panels that are 8cm/3in longer, so that they overlap each other near the middle of the bottle. (This will provide a gap for you to put your hot-water bottle into the cover when you have finished making it.)

STEP 3

Now cut and sew your bear head and paws onto the front panel, just like you did on your blanket (p.34).

STEP 4

Pin the bottom back panel onto the front panel, with the *wrong sides* (the back of the fabric) facing each other. Pin the top back panel in place in the same way. Sew the cover together, all around the outside edges, using Blanket or Straight Stitch.

Yummy Cushions

Stitches: Straight Stitch, Blanket Stitch

Skills: Using a pattern, using pins, appliqué

Materials: Felt: 2 squares for cushion, plus felt and fabric scraps, embroidery thread, buttons, cushion stuffing

STEP 1

Decide on the design you want to put on your yummy cushion, either an ice-cream cone or cupcake. Copy the template patterns (p.68) onto tracing paper, cut them out and pin to your different fabrics and cut out.

STEP 2

Arrange the fabric shapes to make the design. Pin them to one felt square for the front of the cushion. Make sure you put the pieces in the correct order!

STEP 3

Sew your design carefully in place. You can use different stitches for each of the pieces of the design if you like. Add any buttons or beads now too.

Mmmmmmmm! Yummy!

STEP 4

Pin the 2 squares together. Sew around 3 edges and stuff the cushion. Pin the open edge closed to keep the stuffing in, then sew up to finish your yummy cushion! Make another with a different design.

Hanging Hearts

Stitches: Straight Stitch, Blanket Stitch, Slipstitch
Skills: Using a pattern, using pins, sewing on a button, appliqué
Materials: A selection of pretty felts and fabrics, stuffing, ribbons for hanging, buttons to decorate

STEP 1
For each heart, fold your fabric and use the heart pattern (p.69) to trace and then cut out 2 heart shapes from felt or printed fabric.

STEP 2
Now sew on smaller heart shapes, ribbons or buttons, to decorate 1 of the heart pieces.

STEP 3
Now pin both of your heart pieces together, and use Straight Stitch or Blanket Stitch to sew around the edge. Leave a gap to stuff your heart before you finish sewing it up with Slipstitch!

STEP 4
Now sew some ribbon at the top to hang your heart from!

I LOVE making these cool hearts!

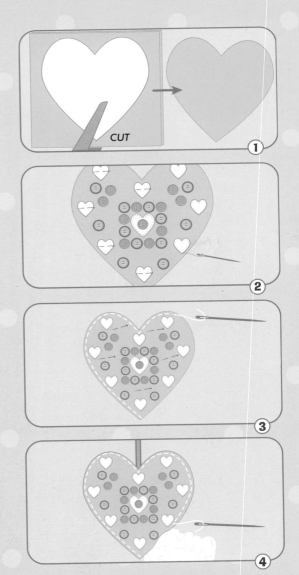

CUT

Cool Zip Cases

Stitches: Backstitch
Skills: Cutting, using pins, appliqué
Materials: Felts and fabrics for the cases, zip, fabrics to decorate

STEP 1

You need a zip the same size as your bag. Cut 2 pieces of fabric the same length as your zip — 1 for each side of your case. Pin your zip along the long edge of 1 piece of the fabric, with the right side of the zip facing the right side of the fabric. Backstitch 1 side of the zip to the fabric.

STEP 2

Pin and then backstitch the other side of the zip onto the second piece of fabric in the same way.

STEP 3

Now decorate your zip case by stitching cool appliqué shapes to it. You can do just 1 side, or both if you prefer!

STEP 4

To sew up the case, open the zip halfway so that you can turn your zip case right sides out later. Position the fabric panels with their right sides together and use Backstitch to sew around the 3 sides. Now turn your zip case right sides out.

Right side of zip face down
Sew
Right side
①

②

③

④

I made a purse to store my money in. What's yours for?

Denim Bag

Stitches: Backstitch

Skills: Cutting, using pins, sewing on a buttton, appliqué

Materials: An old pair of jeans will make two bags, plus ribbon for handle and trims

STEP 1
Cut around the back pocket of an old pair of jeans, making sure you cut through the jeans themselves, so you end up with an entire pocket, ready to turn into a bag.

STEP 2
Cut a piece of ribbon the length of your bag handle, plus 4cm/1½ in.

STEP 3
Sew each end of your ribbon handle to the inside of the pocket fabric. Use a strong stitch like Backstitch and sew in a little square for extra strength.

STEP 4
Now decorate the front of your bag with ribbons, buttons or bows.

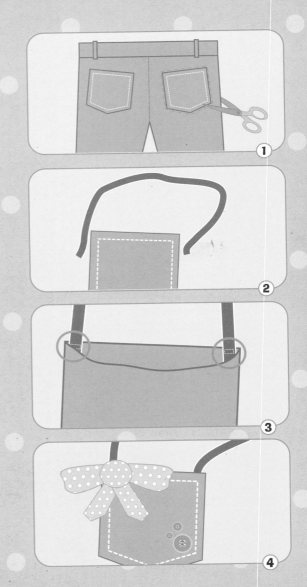

Tissue Monsters

Stitches: Backstitch or Straight Stitch
Skills: Cutting, using pins, appliqué
Materials: Felts and fabrics, googly eyes or buttons, matching thread

STEP 1

Cut out a rectangle of felt or fabric that measures 15cm x 25cm/6 x 10in. Turn the short ends under by about 1cm/½in and sew with Straight Stitch. You can use thread that matches the fabric *or* one that will stand out!

STEP 2

With the right side of the fabric facing up, fold the top and bottom edges towards each other until they meet in the middle. Pin the sides.

STEP 3

Now using Backstitch — as it is stronger — and a thread the same colour as the fabric, sew the sides together, about 1cm (½in) in from the edge.

STEP 4

Turn your tissue monster the right way out and add the face made from coloured scraps of felt decorated with different stitches. Will yours be a scary or a sweet monster?

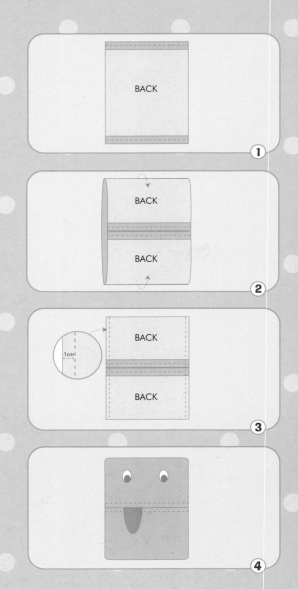

House Needlecase

Stitches: Overstitch, Straight Stitch
Skills: Using a pattern, using pins, appliqué
Materials: Felt in various colours

STEP 1

Place the house pattern (p.70) on a folded piece of felt and cut out. Do not cut along the fold, so that your house shape will be 2 houses joined together at one side. Then cut out the 4 windows, door and roof in other colours.

STEP 2

Overstitch the roof, door and windows to the front of the house.

STEP 3

Now cut another double house shape in a different colour felt for the inside of your needlecase. Place inside the cover and use Straight Stitch to sew the two layers together.

Use the patterns on page 70

STEP 4

Fold the the house over.
Use the inner felt layers for your pins and needles. Now they have a lovely new home!

Birdy Garland

Stitches: Straight Stitch, Blanket Stitch

Skills: Using a pattern, using pins, sewing on a button, appliqué

Materials: Felts and fabrics for the birds, stuffing, buttons to decorate, ribbon for hanging

STEP 1

Fold your piece of fabric so that the right side is facing up. Use the birdy template (p.71) to cut 2 bird shapes from the same piece of fabric. Repeat for each bird, using different fabrics.

STEP 2

Decorate the top layer of each bird, adding eyes, wings and so on.

STEP 3

Now pin and sew each bird together, stuffing them before you finish sewing them up. You can use Straight Stitch or Blanket Stitch.

STEP 4

Now spread out your ribbon and pin your birds at regular intervals on it, then sew the ribbon onto the back of each birdy.

Snuggly Slippers

Stitches: Straight Stitch, Blanket Stitch
Skills: Using a pattern, using pins, appliqué
Materials: Felt, card, googly eyes or buttons

STEP 1

Draw around each of your feet to make a paper pattern for your slipper base. Cut 1 piece of thick card for each foot from this pattern. Next cut 2 pieces of felt for each foot, about 1cm (½in) *bigger* all around than the card.

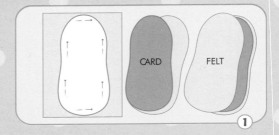

STEP 2

Now use the cat or frog pattern (p.71 and p.72) to cut out 2 of your chosen animal shape. Mark and sew on the animal features now.

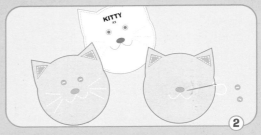

STEP 3

Make a *felt, card and felt* sandwich for the base of each slipper and pin all around the edge. Also position your animal face and pin in place.

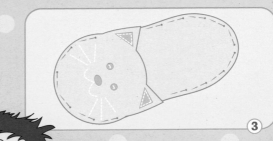

STEP 4

Now use either Blanket or Straight Stitch to sew all around your slipper. Don't forget to add an extra stitch for strength where the animal face joins the slipper base!

I'm making froggy feet !

Book Cover

Stitches: Straight Stitch, Blanket Stitch
Skills: Cutting, using pins, sewing on a button
Materials: Fabric, buttons, trims

STEP 1

To make your cover, first lay your chosen book open flat on your fabric. Mark where to cut, allowing 1cm/½in extra at the *top and bottom*, plus an extra 10cm/4in on each side.

STEP 2

Cut the cover out, put your open book back onto the wrong side of the fabric, wrap the sides of the fabric over your book and pin the top and bottom on each side to make pockets. Remove the book and add any decorative shapes, buttons or bows to the front (like the Cool Zip Cases on page 42).

STEP 3

Sew from one side to the other, first along the top, then along the bottom using Straight or Blanket Stitch. Make sure you sew through both layers of the fabric to make the pockets at each end.

Don't forget to start and finish with a double stitch every time!

STEP 4

Now you can put your book back into its pretty new cover.

Bags of fun!

Stitches: Straight Stitch, Backstitch
Skills: Cutting, using pins, appliqué
Materials: Fabric for bag, fancy trimmings, ribbons, embroidery thread

STEP 1
Cut a long rectangle from a piece of fabric and fold it in half. With the wrong side facing you, fold each end over about 2cm/³/₄in and pin. Sew a line of Straight Stitch along both ends about 1cm/½in away from the folded edge.

STEP 2
Decorate the front of your bag before you sew the rest together, so use stitches, ribbons and appliqué to make it look lovely! Remember to check which way is *up* for both sides of the bag.

STEP 3
Now fold the fabric in half with the right sides together. Pin the edges, then Backstitch along each side 1cm/³/₄in from the edge. Turn bag right sides out.

STEP 4
Cut 2 pieces of ribbon, each about 3 times the width of your bag. Attach a safety pin to the end of 1 piece of ribbon and push it through from 1 folded edge to the other. Tie the ribbon ends together with a knot. Starting at the opposite side of the bag, do the same again with the second ribbon.

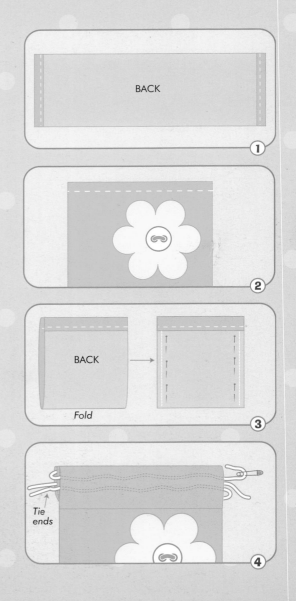

Titchy Teddy Bear

Stitches: Overstitch, Slipstitch
Skills: Using a pattern, using pins
Materials: Felt, stuffing, felt for eyes or nose

STEP 1

Use the patterns (p.74) to cut 2 pieces of felt for the front of your bear and 2 pieces for the back. Cut the first piece, then flip the pattern over to cut the second piece so that it is a mirror image of the first.

STEP 2

Pin the front pieces *wrong sides* together and use Overstitch to sew from the the bottom of the tummy to the top of the head. Pin and sew the back pieces together in the same way, but leave a small gap for stuffing your bear later.

STEP 3

Pin the front and the back pieces, *wrong sides* together. Overstitch all the edges around the bear's body. Next start adding a little stuffing at a time through the gap at the back. Fill the legs, arms and head first then stuff until your bear is full. Close the gap with Slipstitch.

Don't forget to start and finish with a double stitch every time!

STEP 4

Next use bits of felt and decorative stitches for his nose, eyes and mouth. Now he's ready to dress...turn to the next page to make his first outfit!

Titchy Teddy Clothes

Stitches: Straight Stitch
Skills: Using a pattern, using pins, appliqué
Materials: Felt in various colours, buttons and trims to decorate

STEP 1

You can make a jacket or a little dress for your titchy teddy. Look at the teddy clothes patterns on page 74. Does it tell you to *cut 1 (x 1)* or *cut 2 (x 2)* pieces of felt? Make sure you trace and cut the right number of pattern pieces.

STEP 2

Pin the patterns to either 1 or 2 layers of felt and cut out the right number of pieces.

STEP 3

Sew the pattern pieces together using Straight Stitch. Follow Daisy's dots on the patterns to see where to sew up. Don't forget to double stitch at the start and end of each row of stitching!

STEP 4

Now you can decorate your clothes with buttons, ribbons and trims!

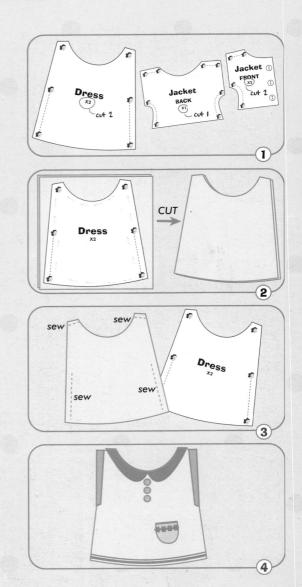

Cupcake Pincushion

Stitches: Straight Stitch, Overstitch
Skills: Using a pattern, using pins, sewing on beads
Materials: Felt squares, embroidery thread, beads, stuffing

STEP 1
Trace off the cupcake patterns (p.68). Cut out
2 cupcake shapes from some coloured felt. Then
cut 1 icing shape from a different coloured felt
or from printed fabric.

STEP 2
If you are using felt, sew some beads onto the
icing. If you are using printed fabric for the icing
you can forget this step.

STEP 3
Pin the 2 layers of felt for the cupcake together.
Pin the icing in place, on top of the 2 layers
of cupcake felt.

STEP 4
Straight stitch around round the cupcake
shape, and through the icing layer too,
and leave a small space so you can
stuff the cupcake then stuff it and
Slipstitch the gap to close it.

Yum! Looks good enough to eat!

Gingerbread Men

Stitches: Straight Stitch, Slipstitch, Overstitch
Skills: Using a pattern, using pins, sewing on buttons
Materials: Brown felt for gingerbread men, googly eyes, ricrac or ribbon, stuffing

STEP 1
Trace off the gingerbread man pattern from page 76. Pin the gingerbread man pattern to 2 layers of felt and cut out. Cut out as many gingerbread men as you want.

STEP 2
Decorate his face with a stitched mouth. Sew on his buttons, ribbon clothes and add his eyes.

STEP 3
Now pin the front and back pieces of your gingerbread man together and sew all around using Straight Stitch. If you'd like to stuff him, leave a gap when stitching, fill him and Slipstitch the gap closed.

STEP 4
Overstitch a ribbon to the back of his head to hang him up with.

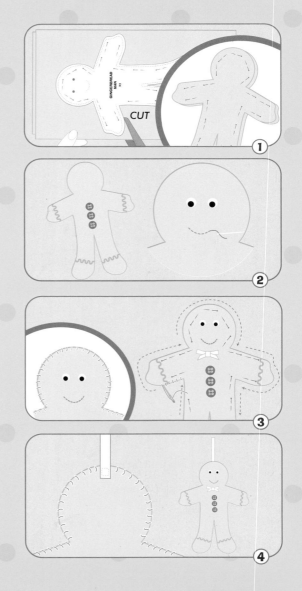

Egg Cosies

Stitches: Blanket Stitch, Straight Stitch
Skills: Using a pattern, using pins, appliqué
Materials: Various felts, fabrics and ribbons

STEP 1

Cut out 2 egg cosy shapes from a piece of felt. Cut out any shapes you want for decorating your egg cosy, such as a bunny (p.77) or a birdy (p.71) or your own pattern, such as a fried egg.

STEP 2

Pin your chosen shapes to the front of each egg cosy. Straight Stitch the shapes to decorate each piece.

STEP 3

Pin both sides of the cosy together. Now Blanket Stitch around the the curved edges.

EGG-CELLENT!!

STEP 4

Now you can put your cosies over your boiled eggs to keep them nice and warm.

Yummy Cushions Patterns

ICING

ICE CREAM CONE

CUPCAKE

ICE CREAM

Hanging Hearts Patterns

LARGE HEART

SMALL HEART

JELLY BEAN

STRAWBERRY

Zip Cases Patterns

Tissue Monsters Patterns

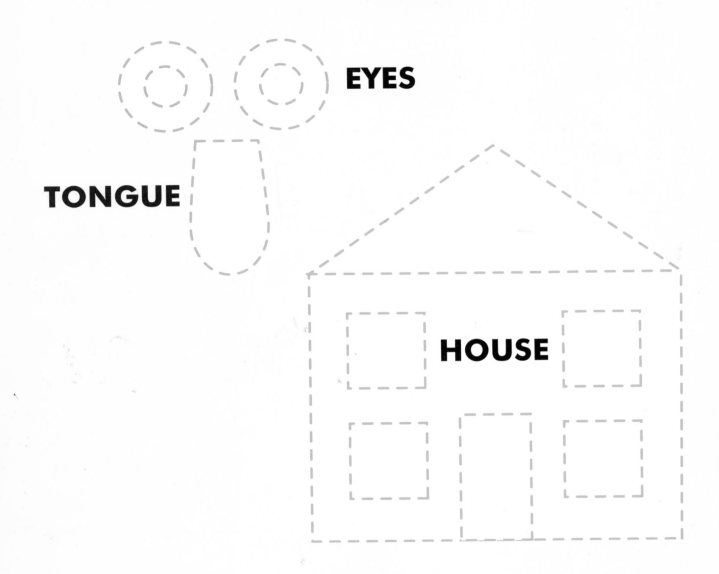

EYES

TONGUE

HOUSE

House Needlecase Patterns

Birdy Garland Pattern

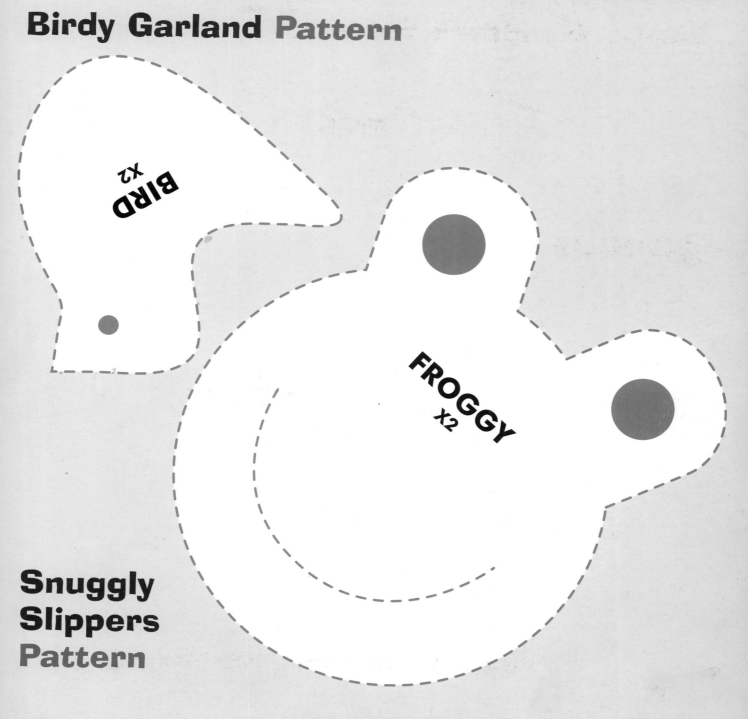

BIRD
X2

FROGGY
X2

Snuggly Slippers Pattern

Snuggly Slippers Pattern

KITTY

FLOWER

Bags of fun,
Book cover,
Flower Brooch Pattern

Titchy Teddy Pattern

BEAR FRONT

BEAR BACK

Teddy Clothes Patterns

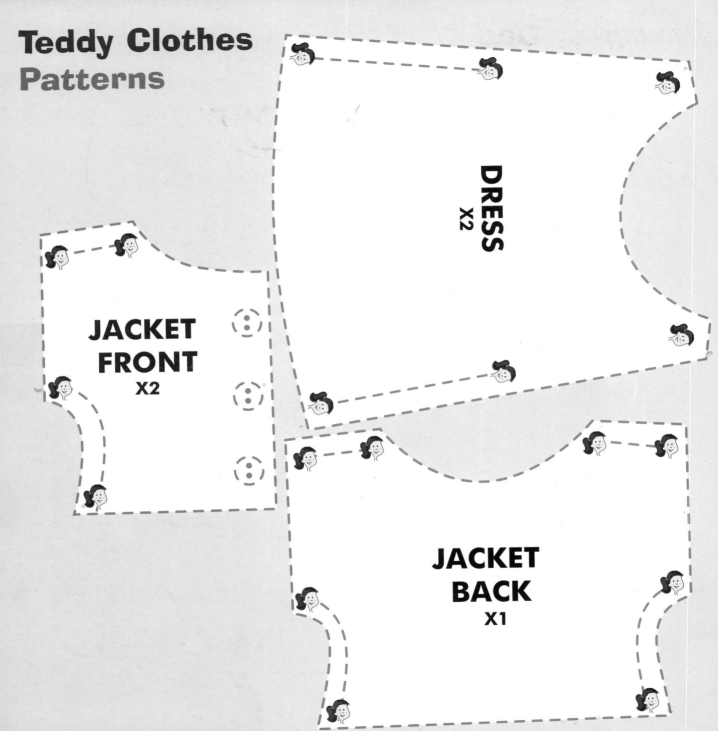

DRESS
X2

JACKET FRONT
X2

JACKET BACK
X1

Draughty Dog
Patterns

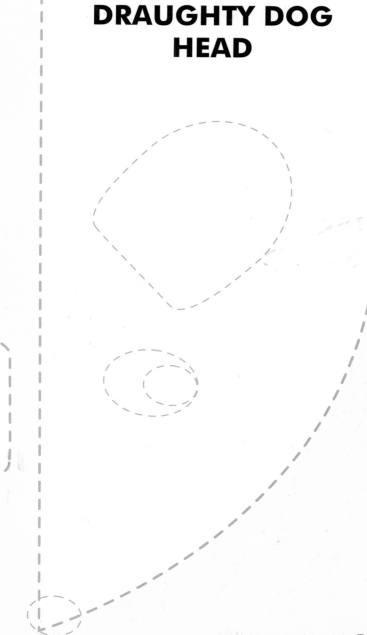

DRAUGHTY DOG HEAD

EAR
X2

Gingerbread Man Pattern

GINGERBREAD
MAN

Bear Blanket & Hot Water Bottle Patterns

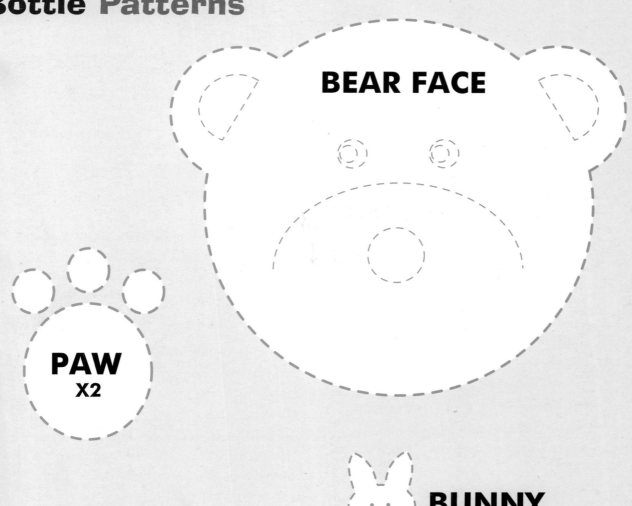

BEAR FACE

PAW
X2

Egg Cosy Pattern

BUNNY

Suppliers and products

The yarns, threads and haberdashery used in this book are supplied by Coats Crafts UK. Their main address is listed below. More detailed lists of stockists can be found on their website.

Coats Crafts UK
Lingfield Point
McMullen Road
Darlington
Co Durham
tel +44 (0)1325 395237

www.coatscrafts.co.uk

Yarns and threads

Coats Cotton sewing thread is for machine and hand stitching, ideal for cotton fabrics.

Coats Duet sewing threads is for machine stitching polyester fabrics.

Anchor Pearl Cotton is ideal for decorative hand stitches.

Anchor Tapisserie Wool is a 100 per cent wool yarn ideal for decorative hand stitches on thicker fabrics, eg. for blanket stitching.

Fabrics

Anchor Style and Filz-it felt is available in A4 sheets in various styles — plain, glitter, patterned or embossed — in a wide range of colours.

Rowan Yarns have a wide range of printed and plain cotton fabrics. Check out the Rowan Yarns website (www.knitrowan.com) for details of stockists.

Haberdashery and equipment

Coats Crafts have a wide range of haberdashery — pins and needles, scissors, fabric marking pencils, tape measures and so on as well as decorative appliqué motifs, beads and buttons, and bag accessories.

Stitchclub

For more information about Stitchclub Sewing Classes and their fantastic online store featuring a huge range of children's sewing supplies and Sew Easy Kits visit:

www.stitchclub.co.uk

Index

A
aliens 30
appliqué 16, 38

B
backstitch 22, 28,
bag charms, monster 30
bag, denim 44
bags of fun 56
beads
    how to sew 17
bear blanket 36
bear hot-water bottle cover 36
bear pattern 77
birdy garland 50
    pattern 71
blanket, bear 34
blanket stitch 21, 34, 52, 54, 66
book cover 54
brooch, flower 32
brooch pin 32
bunny pattern 77
buttons 9
    how to sew on 12

C
cases, zip 42
chain stitch 25
cool zip cases 42
cosies, egg 66
crazy creatures 30
cross stitch 24
cupcake cushions 38
cupcake patterns 68
cupcake pincushions 62
cushions, yummy 38

D
denim bag 44

draughty dog 28
    pattern 75

E
egg cosies 66
embroidery threads

F
fabrics 9
felt 9
    projects with 30, 32, 38, 40,
    48, 52, 60, 62. 64, 66
flower appliqué 56
flower brooch 32
    pattern 72

G
garland, birdy 50
gingerbread men 64
    pattern 76
gingham 24

H
hanging hearts 40
heart patterns 69
hot-water bottle cover 36
house needlecase 48

I
ice-cream cone cushions 38
ice-cream cone patterns 68

J
jelly bean pattern 69

K
key rings, monster 30

M
monsters, key ring 30
monsters, tissue 46

N
needlecase, house 48

pattern 70
needles 7
    how to thread 12

O
overstitch 23

P
patterns
    how to use 15
    for projects 68-77
pincushion, cupcake 62
pins 7
    how to use 14

R
ribbons and trims 9

S
scissors 9
sewing box 8
sewing kit 8
sewing threads 9
slippers, snuggly 52
    pattern 71
slipstitch 23
stitchclub 7
stitches 18
straight stitch 20
strawberry pattern 69

T
tissue monsters 46
    patterns 70
titchy teddy bear 58
    pattern 73
titchy teddy clothes 60
    pattern 74

Z
zip cases 42

Acknowledgments

I hope you enjoyed this book, and had as much fun making the projects as I had designing them!

I'd like to say a huge thanks to everyone at Coats Crafts UK for all the support they have given Stitchclub, and for making this book a reality, especially my editor Susan Berry for her huge amount of hard work putting it all together and answering my thousands of questions with endless patience!

This book, and Stitchclub, just wouldn't have been possible without the most fantastic illustrator, Julie Anson. Her talent and ability to turn my ideas into wonderful and easy to follow illustrations are a constant inspiration and myself, Daisy Doublestitch and Billy Bobbin would like to thank her SEW much!

And most importantly, I'd like to thank the talented team of Stitchclub teachers and every one of their thousands of pupils across the country who attend our Stitchclub classes every week. When I started Stitchclub, my dream was to show a whole new generation of children how much fun sewing can be, so thank you for helping to make that come true!

And finally to Elizabeth McNicol, my gran and favourite stitcher, without whom none of this would have happened. I miss you every day, and this book is for you.

Keep stitching!

Alison